INSPIRATIONAL SHORT HOCKEY STORIES

THE INCREDIBLE STORIES OF 12 HOCKEY
CHAMPIONS, DESIGNED TO INSPIRE AND CAPTIVATE
THE HEARTS OF YOUNG HOCKEY FANS AND
ASPIRING ATHLETES WORLDWIDE

ELVIN CREATIONS

ELVIN CREATIONS

contained within this document, including, but not limited to—errors, omissions, or inaccuracies

CONTENTS

Introduction   7

1. Bobby Orr   9
2. Mario Lemieux   17
3. Gordie Howe   27
4. Maurice "Rocket" Richard   35
5. Jean Béliveau   43
6. Sidney Crosby   51
7. Dominik Hasek   59
8. Wayne Gretzky   65
9. Peter Forsber   73
10. Alexander Ovechkin   81
11. Connor McDavid   89
12. Auston Matthews   97

Conclusion   103

INTRODUCTION

In the exhilarating world of hockey, where the clash of blades and the thunder of the puck echo the spirit of resilience and the pursuit of greatness, lies a treasure trove of remarkable stories. Within these pages, you will embark on a journey of inspiration, courage, and unwavering determination, guided by the extraordinary tales of some of the most legendary figures in the history of the sport.

Welcome to a world where the ice becomes a canvas for dreams, and where every stride embodies the unwritten code of perseverance. In this book, we delve into the lives of hockey's finest, from the dazzling saves of Dominik Hasek to the lightning-fast plays of Connor McDavid and the remarkable journey of Auston Matthews. Through their trials, triumphs, and unwavering passion for the game, we unravel the threads of resilience and perseverance that bind their stories together, weaving a tapestry of inspiration for every young dreamer, athlete, and enthusiast.

Join us as we explore the depths of dedication, the power of teamwork, and the transformative spirit that propels these iconic athletes toward greatness. Let their tales serve as a beacon of hope, igniting the flames of ambition within each reader, and guiding them on a path of self-discovery, perseverance, and unwavering commitment to their own aspirations.

Through the triumphs and tribulations of these hockey heroes, may you find the courage to chase your own dreams, the strength to overcome every obstacle, and the unwavering belief that within every young heart lies the potential for greatness.

Let the journey begin.

1

BOBBY ORR

"Success is not just about talent; it's about hard work, dedication, and the will to win."

In the annals of ice hockey history, few names shine as brightly as that of Bobby Orr. Born on March 20, 1948, in Parry Sound, Ontario, Canada, Robert Gordon Orr would go on to become one of the most iconic and influential figures in the world of sports. His journey from a small Canadian town to hockey superstardom is a tale of remarkable talent, perseverance, and an unwavering commitment to excellence.

The First Days on the Frozen Pond

Bobby Orr's passion for hockey began at an early age, as it does for many Canadians. His father, Doug Orr, was instrumental in instilling in him a love of the sport. Bobby spent many hours improving his abilities and building a profound connection to the game on the frozen ponds of Parry Sound.

Orr left home at the age of 14 to join the Oshawa Generals, an Ontario junior hockey team. This was the start of his formal hockey career, and it didn't take long for his tremendous skill to shine through. Orr was a defenseman with a distinct combination of speed, agility, and offensive ability that separated him apart from his colleagues.

Boston's Rising Star

Bobby Orr's life would take a dramatic change in 1966 when he was selected first overall in the NHL Amateur Draft by the Boston Bruins. He made his NHL debut at the age of 18 during the 1966-67 season, instantly establishing himself as a budding talent.

Orr's contribution to the game was innovative. He reinvented the job of the defenseman, becoming not only a defensive stalwart but also a powerful attacking force. His ability to move the puck with precision and speed across the ice, paired with his remarkable vision, allowed him to tally up points at an incredible rate for a defenseman.

Orr made history by being the first defender in NHL history to win the league scoring title in 1969-70, earning an incredible 120 points. He also earned the Hart Trophy as the league's most valuable player, becoming him the league's youngest winner at the time.

In search of the elusive Stanley Cup

Despite his individual achievement, Orr's ultimate ambition was to win the Stanley Cup, professional hockey's most prized award. Orr was determined to alter that, as the Bruins had not won a championship in almost three decades.

The tipping moment came when Orr led the Bruins to the Stanley Cup Finals in 1969-70. He not only clinched the victory but also carved his name into hockey history with a thrilling overtime goal in Game 4. With the goal, the Bruins won their first Stanley Cup in 29 years, and Orr was named the Conn Smythe Trophy winner as the playoffs' most valuable player.

The next season, Orr and the Bruins won the Stanley Cup again, cementing his place in hockey history. He proceeded to dominate the game, earning Norris Trophies year after year as the greatest defenseman.

Physical Costs and Persistence

Despite his great accomplishments, Orr's career was defined by a never-ending fight with injury. He had many knee operations, which reduced the amount of games he could play. Despite this, his dedication to the game and his teammates was unwavering.

Orr left Boston in 1976 to join the Chicago Blackhawks, seeking a fresh start and the opportunity to continue playing at the top level. However, his knees continued to bother him, and he resigned from professional hockey at the age of 30 in 1978.

Orr's body had taken a toll, but his soul remained intact. He fought through the agony, demonstrating amazing resilience and passion to the sport he loved.

Life After Hockey

While his playing career was done, Bobby Orr's influence in the world of hockey was far from over. He went on to have a successful career as a player agent, then as a coach and executive, while remaining intimately connected in the game he loved.

Off the ice, Orr has been a charitable force, leveraging his celebrity and clout to make an impact in his neighborhood and beyond. He has been a vocal supporter of children's concerns and education, actively donating to organizations that help young people flourish.

The Inspirational Legacy

Bobby Orr's path from a small child skating on frozen ponds to becoming a hockey icon is an inspiring one. His unrivaled talent and relentless commitment have left an indelible imprint on the sport of ice hockey.

Orr's legacy goes beyond the rink, reminding us that success is defined not just by personal accomplishments, but also by the impact we have on others and the good change we can effect in our communities. His dedication to giving back and assisting those in need serves as an example for both athletes and individuals.

Bobby Orr's name will long be associated with brilliance in a sport where legends are born and cherished.

His narrative exemplifies the power of enthusiasm, determination, and perseverance.

"Remember that the journey is just as important as the destination. Enjoy every moment and savor the experiences along the way."

What did we learn from him?

We may learn essential lessons about life and sports from Bobby Orr's illustrious career. His persistent dedication, extraordinary skill, and game-changing approach have left an indelible mark on the world of hockey and beyond. Orr's unwavering pursuit of perfection, along with his unique style of play, transformed the position of defenseman in the NHL and encouraged a generation of young players to push the limits of what was considered possible. On and off the ice, his leadership embodied the traits of honesty, sportsmanship, and humility, serving as a strong reminder of the value of character and persistence in attaining one's goals. Through devotion, enthusiasm, and a commitment to perfection, Orr's everlasting legacy continues to inspire others to strive for greatness, embrace innovation, and leave a lasting impression on their respective industries.

Achievements :

Calder Trophy: Bobby Orr won the Calder Memorial Trophy as the NHL's Rookie of the Year in the 1966-67 season, beginning his career with a strong impact.

Hart Trophy (3 times): Orr was awarded the Hart Memorial Trophy as the league's Most Valuable Player three times during his career in 1970, 1971, and 1972. His ability to dominate games from the defense position was unprecedented.

Norris Trophy (8 times): Orr won the James Norris Memorial Trophy as the NHL's best defenseman a record eight times in consecutive years from 1968 to 1975.

Art Ross Trophy (2 times): In an extraordinary feat, Orr became the only defenseman in NHL history to lead the league in scoring, winning the Art Ross Trophy in 1970 and 1975.

Stanley Cup Championships (2 times): Bobby Orr played a pivotal role in leading the Boston Bruins to two Stanley Cup championships in 1970 and 1972. His iconic goal in overtime during the 1970 Stanley Cup Final secured the championship and remains one of the most iconic moments in NHL history.

International Achievements:

Canada Cup (2 times): Orr represented Canada in the 1976 and 1981 Canada Cup tournaments, contributing to two championship victories for his country.

Legacy and Honors:

Hall of Fame: Bobby Orr was inducted into the Hockey Hall of Fame in 1979, solidifying his status as one of the greatest players in the history of the sport.

Number Retirement: The Boston Bruins retired Orr's jersey number 4 as a tribute to his outstanding contributions to the team and the game.

Statue in Boston: Outside the TD Garden in Boston, a bronze statue of Bobby Orr celebrates his iconic goal and lasting impact on the Bruins and the city.

Orr's Influence on the Game: Bobby Orr's style of play revolutionized the role of defensemen in hockey, emphasizing offensive contributions from the blue line. His legacy continues to influence the way the game is played today.

2

MARIO LEMIEUX

"The only way a kid is going to practice is if it's total fun for him... and it was for me."

A little boy's fate was carved on the frozen ponds that extended as far as the eye could see in the tranquil village of Ville-Émard, situated in the heart of Quebec. Mario Lemieux initially laced up his skates in this inconspicuous corner of Canada, his passion for hockey fueled by the coolness of the winter air and the rhythmic beat of sticks striking the puck. Little did the world know that from these modest beginnings would emerge a hockey prodigy—one whose name would become associated with brilliance. This is the narrative of a youngster who dared to dream, Mario Lemieux's story.

Early Years and ascension to Stardom

Mario Lemieux was born in Montreal, Quebec, on October 5, 1965. Growing up in a humble home in the mining village of Ville-Émard presented many hardships. But it was clear from an early age that Lemieux possessed a rare gift—a remarkable skill for hockey.

His quick climb through the levels of Canadian junior hockey was remarkable. Lemieux shattered scoring records and displayed his unearthly abilities while playing for the Laval Voisins in the Quebec Major Junior Hockey League. His efforts piqued the interest of NHL scouts, and he was on track to be the first overall choice in the 1984 NHL Draft.

Era of the Pittsburgh Penguins

The Pittsburgh Penguins won the NHL draft lottery in 1984, gaining Mario Lemieux's rights. It was a watershed moment for both the franchise and the young star.

Lemieux had an instant impact on the ice. He scored his first NHL goal on his first shot, a hint of things to come. He was a scoring phenomenon, demonstrating a unique mix of size, speed, and scoring ability in the league. The NHL has found its next big thing.

Lemieux earned the Art Ross Trophy as the league's best scorer in his second season, accumulating 141 points. It was the start of a long list of honors and achievements that would define his career. He would win the scoring championship six times in a row.

Pursuing Greatness and Overcoming Obstacles

Despite his early success, Lemieux faced several obstacles both on and off the court. Injuries hampered his career, with back problems being especially troublesome. Nonetheless, Lemieux's fortitude was unyielding. He underwent many operations and endured excruciating agony in order to continue playing the game he adored.

During the 1988-89 season, Lemieux had one of his most memorable games. Despite missing 21 games due to injury, he scored 85 goals, which is the second-highest total in NHL history. It was a testimonial to his scoring skill and perseverance in the face of adversity.

But it wasn't simply Lemieux's scoring ability that distinguished him. He was a complete player who was frequently likened to Wayne Gretzky. His vision and playmaking abilities were exceptional, and he was a two-time Hart Trophy winner as the league's Most Valuable Player.

Glory in the Stanley Cup and Leadership

Despite all of his individual accomplishments, Lemieux's ultimate ambition was to win the Stanley Cup. He led the Pittsburgh Penguins to consecutive championships in 1991 and 1992, receiving the Conn Smythe Trophy as playoff MVP on both occasions. It was the pinnacle achievement for a player widely regarded as one of the finest to ever put on skates.

Lemieux's influence stretched beyond the ice. He bought the Pittsburgh Penguins in 1993, when the team was facing bankruptcy and relocation. His dedication to preserving hockey in Pittsburgh, as well as the city's appreciation for his efforts, endeared him to fans even more.

The Unthinkable Return

Mario Lemieux faced his most difficult assignment yet in 1993, at the pinnacle of his career. Hodgkin's lymphoma, a kind of cancer, was discovered in him. The hockey world was shocked and supportive of his choice to leave the game to receive therapy.

Surprisingly, Lemieux returned to the ice just months later after finishing radiation therapy. His recovery was nothing short of spectacular. He had a goal and an assist in his first game back. It was a moment that went beyond sports, stirring people well beyond the confines of the rink.

Lemieux earned the scoring championship with 160 points despite playing only 60 games that season. He received the Lester B. Pearson Award as the NHL's most outstanding player as voted on by his teammates.

The Legacy of the Second Retirement

Mario Lemieux retired for the first time in 1997, citing continuing health difficulties. But his passion for the game never faded. He returned to the Penguins as a player-owner in 2000, lacing up his skates once more to set an example. His guidance and mentoring of a new generation of players left an unforgettable imprint on the team.

In his final season, Lemieux passed the baton to Jaromir Jagr, a young player who would go on to become one of the league's brightest lights. It was a fitting finish to a spectacular career, as Lemieux demonstrated his selflessness and dedication to the team once more.

The Influence of Post-Retirement

Mario Lemieux continues to have an impact in the hockey world after his second retirement in 2006. He remained an owner of the Penguins and was instrumental in the development of the team's new facility, the Consol Energy Center (now PPG Paints facility).

Lemieux's influence went beyond the Penguins. His foundation, the Mario Lemieux Foundation, raised millions of dollars for cancer research and patient care. He utilized his personal cancer struggle to inspire and help others who were experiencing similar problems.

"Don't let anyone tell you that you can't do something. If you have a dream, go for it."

What did we learn from him?

Mario Lemieux's life and career embody resilience, determination, and leadership. From humble beginnings in Ville-Émard, Quebec, he rose to become an iconic figure in hockey history. Lemieux's battle with injuries and cancer showcases his unwavering perseverance. His remarkable comeback from cancer treatment to winning scoring titles highlights the indomitable human spirit.

Lemieux's leadership extended beyond the rink as he became a player-owner and mentor, leaving an indelible mark on the Pittsburgh Penguins and the NHL. His charitable foundation exemplifies the importance of giving back to the community, particularly in the fight against cancer.

Above all, Mario Lemieux's journey serves as a powerful source of inspiration. It teaches us that with talent, hard work, and self-belief, dreams are attainable, and adversity can be overcome. His legacy continues to inspire generations, reminding us that greatness is not just about personal achievements but also about making a meaningful impact on others' lives.

Achievements:

NHL Debut: Mario Lemieux made his NHL debut on October 11, 1984, for the Pittsburgh Penguins, immediately making an impact by scoring a goal on his first shot in his first game.

Calder Trophy: In his rookie season (1984-85), Lemieux won the Calder Memorial Trophy as the NHL's Rookie of the Year.

Scoring Titles: He led the NHL in scoring and won the Art Ross Trophy six times during his career (1985-86, 1986-87, 1987-88, 1988-89, 1991-92, and 1992-93).

Stanley Cup Championships: Lemieux led the Pittsburgh Penguins to Stanley Cup championships in 1991 and 1992, winning the Conn Smythe Trophy as the playoff MVP on both occasions.

The "Five Goals, Five Ways" Game: On Decemberx 31, 1988, Lemieux achieved a rare feat by scoring five goals in five different ways (even-strength, power-play, shorthanded, penalty shot, and empty-net) in a single game against the New Jersey Devils.

Multiple 100-Point Seasons: He recorded six seasons with 100 or more points during his career, solidifying his status as one of the NHL's greatest scorers.

Ownership of the Pittsburgh Penguins: Lemieux purchased the Pittsburgh Penguins in 1999 and became the first former player to own an NHL team.

The Comeback: After battling Hodgkin's lymphoma, Lemieux made an inspirational comeback in 1993, returning to the ice and leading the league in scoring.

Lester B. Pearson Award: He was awarded the Lester B. Pearson Award (now the Ted Lindsay Award) as the NHL's most outstanding player, as voted by his fellow players, three times (1985-86, 1987-88, and 1992-93).

Hockey Hall of Fame: Mario Lemieux was inducted into the Hockey Hall of Fame in 1997, solidifying his legacy as one of the greatest players in the history of the sport.

3

GORDIE HOWE

"You've got to be a man to play hockey for a living,
but you've got to have a lot of little boy in you, too."

One name stands out in the annals of hockey history as an everlasting emblem of brilliance, passion, and love for the game: Gordie Howe, lovingly known as "Mr. Hockey." His incredible journey from a tiny village in Saskatchewan, Canada, to becoming one of the best players in the National Hockey League (NHL) is proof of passion, tenacity, and the indomitable human spirit.

Early Days in Floral, Saskatchewan

Gordon "Gordie" Howe was born on March 31, 1928, in Floral, Saskatchewan, a small agricultural hamlet. It was a tough winter environment, and the frozen ponds were the community's lifeblood. A young Gordie began to skate on those frozen ponds, teetering precariously on his elder sister's cast-off skates, his passion for the game kindled by the simple delight of gliding on ice.

A celebrity was formed from those humble origins. Gordie's natural aptitude and enthusiasm for hockey were obvious from an early age. In pickup games, he refined his talents, frequently battling against older and more experienced players, acquiring the tenacity and perseverance that would define his remarkable career.

Era of the Detroit Red Wings

Gordie Howe's ambitions came true in 1946, when he joined the Detroit Red Wings at the age of 18. It was the start of a five-decade career, an incredible achievement in and of itself.

Howe had an instant impact on the ice. He distinguished himself by combining remarkable abilities with a commanding physical presence. He soon rose to prominence in the league thanks to his strong shot, excellent passing, and exceptional hockey IQ. He was an important component of the Red Wings' success, helping them win four Stanley Cups in the 1950s.

The Manufacturing Process

Howe's collaboration with fellow Red Wings stalwarts Sid Abel and Ted Lindsay resulted in the well-known "Production Line." During the 1950s, these triumvirate dominated the NHL, with Howe leading the league in scoring and receiving multiple awards. He was a force to be reckoned with because of his ability to score goals with both skill and brutality.

Perseverance in the Face of Adversity

Gordie Howe's journey was not without difficulties. In a collision with Toronto Maple Leafs defenseman Ted "Teeder" Kennedy in 1950, he sustained a catastrophic head injury. It was a moment that could have destroyed his career, but Howe fought back with tenacity. He returned to the rink while wearing a specially built helmet.

His longevity demonstrated Howe's extraordinary work ethic and passion to the game. He played in the NHL until the age of 52, a monument to his fitness and undying love of the game.

The Gamer's Gentleman

Gordie Howe was recognized for his modesty and sportsmanship off the rink. He personified what it meant to be a real gentleman of the game. His devotion to fans, compassion to teammates, and respect for opponents all left a lasting imprint on the hockey world.

Inspiration and Legacies

Gordie Howe's legacy transcends numbers and records. With his passion, work ethic, and love for the game, he inspired generations of gamers. He demonstrated that success may be attained not just through talent but also through tenacity and unshakable dedication to one's cause.

His influence extended beyond the rink. Howe's charitable contributions included work with children's hospitals, demonstrating his compassion and willingness to give back to the community.

The Last Goodbye

Gordie Howe departed from the NHL in 1971, but his passion for the game never faded. In a stunning turn of events, he returned to professional hockey in 1973 to play for the Houston Aeros in the World Hockey Association (WHA) with his sons, Mark and Marty. The "Howe Family" line became an iconic representation of family and hockey.

Gordie Howe played his last NHL season with the Hartford Whalers in 1979, once again shattering records.owcasing his enduring love for the game.

What did we learn from him?

We may learn from Gordie Howe that a tireless pursuit of one's passions, along with steadfast devotion, can lead to extraordinary results. His everlasting love of hockey, as well as his ability to endure in the face of adversity, including career-threatening injuries, teach us the value of perseverance and tenacity.

Gordie Howe's professional career lasted into his early 50s, demonstrating the importance of maintaining physical and mental condition as we age. On and off the field, his sportsmanship and humility serve as reminders of the importance of fair play and respect for others.

Furthermore, his dedication to family and collaboration, as seen by playing alongside his boys, emphasizes the significance of developing strong ties and working jointly toward common goals. Finally, his legacy of giving back to the community pushes us to use our success and influence to improve the lives of others.

Achievements:

Longevity: Howe played professional hockey for an astonishing 32 seasons, earning him the nickname "Mr. Hockey." He was the only player to compete in the NHL in five different decades.

Most Games Played in the NHL: Until his record was surpassed by Mark Messier, Gordie Howe held the record for the most games played in the NHL, with a total of 1,767 games.

Most Seasons Played in the NHL: Howe also held the record for the most seasons played in the NHL, with 26 seasons in the league.

Scoring Titles: He won the Art Ross Trophy as the NHL's leading scorer six times (1951, 1952, 1953, 1954, 1957, and 1963).

Most Goals in a Career: At the time of his retirement, Howe held the record for the most career goals in the NHL, with 801 goals.

Hart Trophies: He won the Hart Trophy as the league's Most Valuable Player six times (1952, 1953, 1957, 1958, 1960, and 1963).

Stanley Cup Championships: While with the Detroit Red Wings, Howe won four Stanley Cup championships (1950, 1952, 1954, and 1955).

All-Star Appearances: He was selected to 23 NHL All-Star Games, showcasing his consistent excellence over two decades.

Hall of Fame Induction: Gordie Howe was inducted into the Hockey Hall of Fame in 1972, solidifying his status as one of the greatest players in the history of the sport.

These achievements not only reflect his incredible talent and skill but also his longevity, consistency, and impact on the game of hockey. Gordie Howe's legacy as one of the greatest players of all time is firmly established through these remarkable milestones.

"When you're playing the game, the game is the only thing that matters. But winning or losing doesn't matter in the big scheme of things."

4

MAURICE "ROCKET" RICHARD

"When you start believing in yourself, you start believing in possibilities."

There is a name in the pantheon of hockey superstars that shines brighter than most—a name that conjures visions of blazing speed, unrivaled scoring power, and an uncompromising devotion to perfection. Maurice "Rocket" Richard is the name of a man whose journey from the streets of Montreal to the hallowed ice of the NHL elevated him to the status of a symbol of passion, tenacity, and the indomitable human spirit.

Early Years and Lowly Beginnings

Maurice Richard was born on August 4, 1921, in the working-class area of Hochelaga-Maisonneuve in Montreal, Quebec, into a culture where hockey was more than a sport; it was a way of life. Young Maurice initially laced up his skates in the Richard family's humble house, hovering on the verge of financial ruin, but it was on the outdoor rinks of Montreal's harsh winters that his love for the game truly ignited.

Richard, the ninth of ten children, had to deal with the challenges of a crowded home and insufficient finances. Nonetheless, it was under these confines that his love of hockey blossomed. Onésime Richard, Maurice's father, was instrumental in developing his son's potential, constructing a temporary rink in the backyard and handcrafting a wooden stick that would become an extension of the young boy's ambitions.

The Journey to the Canadiens

Maurice Richard's path to the National Hockey League was not without stumbling blocks. He wasn't the biggest player on the rink, standing at 5 feet 10 inches and weighing roughly 170 pounds, but he had something far more powerful—blazing speed, a furious work ethic, and an unequaled ability to score goals. These qualities did not go unnoticed, and at the age of 20, he made his NHL debut with the Montreal Canadiens in 1942.

His playing style was energizing and revolutionary. Richard's speed gave him the nickname "Rocket," which would live on in the annals of hockey history. He embodied what it meant to be a Canadian—a player who donned the famous red sweater with skill, tenacity, and unflinching devotion.

The Scoring Device

Rocket Richard had an instant influence on the game. He led the NHL in goal scoring on a constant basis and was the first player in history to score 50 goals in a single season, accomplishing this accomplishment in just 50 games during the 1944-45 season. This record-breaking effort cemented his place as one of the game's all-time leading scorers.

But Richard was much more than a goal scorer. He was a tough competitor who set a good example. His on-ice energy encouraged his colleagues, and his unflinching devotion to victory became the benchmark by which the Canadiens were evaluated.

Triumphs and setbacks

Rocket Richard's path was not without its difficulties and trials. He endured persistent checks and intimidation from opponents who attempted to negate his scoring power in an age when the game was played with tremendous violence. Despite this, he held firm, unfazed by hardship.

During the 1954-55 season, Richard experienced one of the most defining events in his career—and in the history of hockey. A tense incident during a game against the Boston Bruins resulted to Richard hitting an official. The subsequent suspension of Richard for the remainder of the regular season and playoffs infuriated Canadiens supporters, resulting in the notorious Richard Riot. The riot reflected Richard's great connection with the people of Montreal, who considered him as more than simply a hockey star, but as a symbol of their own difficulties and aspirations.

Rocket Richard persisted in the face of adversity. He returned to the rink with zeal, guiding the Canadiens to the Stanley Cup in 1956. It was a triumphant moment that exemplified his tenacity and the unshakeable attitude that defined his career.

Inspiration and Legacies

Mauricio "Rocket" Richard's contribution to the game of hockey goes beyond records and statistics. With his lightning-fast speed, work ethic, and ability to produce under pressure, he inspired generations of athletes. His legacy extended beyond the rink, as he became a cultural figure in Quebec and a source of pride for French Canadians.

His legacy is proof that greatness is decided not just by physical size but also by the intensity of one's passion, the depth of one's dedication, and the unflinching belief in one's ability. Richard's journey from the streets of Montreal to the summit of hockey is an encouragement to anybody attempting to overcome obstacles.

Achievements:

Goal-Scoring Records: Richard was the first player in NHL history to score 50 goals in a single season, achieving this milestone in the 1944-45 season in just 50 games. He led the league in goals five times during his career.

Stanley Cup Championships: Richard won eight Stanley Cup championships with the Montreal Canadiens during the 1940s and 1950s (1944, 1946, 1953, 1956, 1957, 1958, 1959, and 1960).

Hart Trophy: He was awarded the Hart Trophy as the NHL's Most Valuable Player twice, in 1947 and 1958.

First Team All-Star Selections: Richard was named a First Team All-Star at right wing ten times during his career.

All-Star Game Appearances: He was selected to play in the NHL All-Star Game on 14 occasions.

Consistency: Richard scored 30 or more goals in a season 14 times during his career, showcasing his remarkable consistency as a goal scorer.

Legacy and Recognition: He remains an iconic figure in hockey history, and the NHL has honored his legacy by naming the Maurice "Rocket" Richard Trophy for the league's top goal scorer.

Cultural Icon: In Quebec, Richard's cultural significance and impact on the French Canadian community cannot be overstated. He became a symbol of cultural pride and resilience.

These achievements, both in terms of individual accolades and team success, solidify Maurice "Rocket" Richard's status as one of the greatest players in the history of the NHL and an enduring icon in the world of hockey.

What did we learn from him?

We may learn from Maurice "Rocket" Richard that perseverance, passion, and unshakable devotion can lead to amazing accomplishment. His path from a poor area to becoming a hockey icon exemplifies the power of pursuing one's hobbies with zeal and tenacity. Richard's perseverance in the face of adversity, such as suspension and physical problems, shows us the value of never giving up on our dreams.

He led by example, encouraging his teammates and setting high expectations for himself. Richard's cultural pride and effect as a cultural figure in Quebec demonstrate the importance of proudly and passionately embracing one's background. His legacy lives on, reminding us that greatness can be attained through hard effort, self-belief, and an unflinching pursuit of our ambitions. Essentially, Maurice "Rocket" Richard's life narrative serves as a light of hope, perseverance, and inspiration for future generations

---

"Never give up, because you never know if the next try is going to be the one that works."

5

JEAN BÉLIVEAU

"I have always believed that if you give 100%, it's impossible to not feel pride in your effort."

Few names in hockey history resound with the same grace, nobility, and talent as Jean Béliveau. His journey from a small town in Quebec to the pinnacle of the sport is a story of not just athletic excellence but also of leadership, character, and the embodiment of hockey's finest values.

Beginnings & Early Years

Jean Arthur Béliveau was born on August 31, 1931, in Trois-Rivières, Quebec, into a culture where hockey was more than simply a game; it was a way of life. Béliveau showed an instinctive passion for the sport at a young age, refining his talents on frozen ponds and rinks in his hometown. His family, like many others in Quebec, had a profound affection for the game, and it was inside this familial devotion that Jean's adventure began.

Béliveau's skill was evident as a youth. Scouts were drawn to his extraordinary abilities as a centerman, and it wasn't long before he was recruited by the Quebec Citadelles, a junior hockey team. This was the start of a career that would propel him to legendary status.

Era of the Montreal Canadiens

Jean Béliveau received an offer that would change the path of his life in 1950: a contract with the Montreal Canadiens, one of the NHL's most legendary organizations. However, the road to the NHL was not without its difficulties. Both the Canadiens and the Quebec Aces put pressure on Béliveau. The Canadiens' unrelenting pursuit of their prized prospect eventually paid off, as Béliveau donned the famous Canadiens uniform in 1953.

Béliveau demonstrated an incredible ability to control the game from the time he walked onto the NHL rink. He was a unique mix of height, ability, and elegance, standing 6 feet 3 inches and 205 pounds. His graceful style of play, which included smooth stickhandling, precise passing, and a powerful shot, established him as a force to be reckoned with.

Béliveau's ability to score was apparent. He was noted for his clutch efforts during postseason games and led the NHL in scoring on many occasions. His 10 Stanley Cup titles with the Canadiens were a tribute to his ability to thrive when it meant the most.

Character and Leadership

Jean Béliveau was a leader in every meaning of the term, aside from his on-ice skill. In 1961, he was chosen captain of the Canadiens, a position he would maintain for the next decade. Beyond the rink, Béliveau was recognized as a mentor to younger players and a source of inspiration to his colleagues.

Not just his abilities, but also his personality, distinguished Béliveau. He was known as the "gentleman of hockey" because of his sportsmanship, modesty, and love for the game. His actions on and off the rink made him a well-liked figure in the hockey world, as well as a role model for aspiring players.

The Lasting Impression

Jean Béliveau's influence on the game of hockey lasted well after his playing career. He shifted into an executive job with the Montreal Canadiens after retiring as a player in 1971, where he continued to contribute to the team's success. He remained a renowned figure in Montreal, and his presence at games inspired both fans and players.

Béliveau was elected into the Hockey Hall of Fame in 1972, solidifying his place as one of the sport's all-time greats. The Canadiens retired his jersey number, 4, an honor reserved for the franchise's most renowned players.

Béliveau's influence extended beyond the hockey community. He was a philanthropist, devoting his time and money to charity endeavors and improving the lives of others. His dedication to giving back mirrored his conviction in the value of leveraging one's success to help others.

Gentleman's Gentleman

Jean Béliveau's life narrative exemplifies the principles that characterize not only hockey, but the human spirit as well. His rise from obscurity to the NHL, as well as his extraordinary skill, leadership, and unshakeable character, made him a great sports star.

Béliveau's impact lives on in hockey fans' hearts, teammates' memories, and the inspiration he brought to future generations of players. He was more than simply a hockey player; he was a symbol of grace, modesty, and excellence—a personification of the sport's best attributes.

What did we learn from him?

Jean Béliveau's life teaches important truths that touch individuals from all walks of life. His path from a modest community to hockey superstar exemplifies the elements that characterize greatness.With elegance, Béliveau showed us the essence of perfection. His ice abilities were matched by his humility and sportsmanship. He demonstrated that genuine greatness does not need the sacrifice of character.Béliveau demonstrated leadership via his deeds as captain of the Montreal Canadiens. His passion, work ethic, and respect for teammates and opponents established an example to which others should aspire, illustrating that leadership is not about titles but about setting an example.

Integrity was at the heart of his personality. Béliveau's constant devotion to honor, whether in successes and tragedies, teaches us that our most significant asset is our character. He was a philanthropist outside of the rink, demonstrating that success is most valuable when shared with others. His dedication to give back serves as a reminder of the powerful effect one person can have on society.

Jean Béliveau's legacy motivates us to strive for greatness, to be humble in our achievement, and to be resilient in the face of adversity. His path from a tiny village to hockey success demonstrates how determination and a never-say-die attitude can help us overcome enormous obstacles.In summary, Béliveau's life teaches us the lasting virtues of character, leadership, and humility, as well as the immense effect one person can have on the world, both inside and outside the area of spousal relationships.

Achievements:

Stanley Cup Championships: Béliveau was part of the Montreal Canadiens during one of the most successful eras in the team's history. He won the Stanley Cup an impressive 10 times during his career (1956, 1957, 1958, 1959, 1960, 1965, 1966, 1968, 1969, and 1971).

Hart Trophy: He was awarded the Hart Trophy as the NHL's Most Valuable Player twice, in 1956 and 1964, underscoring his impact on the league.

Art Ross Trophy: Béliveau also received the Art Ross Trophy as the NHL's leading scorer in 1956 and 1959, showcasing his scoring prowess.

All-Star Selections: He was named a First Team All-Star on six occasions and played in the NHL All-Star Game numerous times.

Leadership as Canadiens Captain: Béliveau was the captain of the Canadiens for a decade, demonstrating his leadership on and off the ice.

Legacy and Recognition: He was inducted into the Hockey Hall of Fame in 1972, solidifying his status as one of the sport's all-time greats. The Montreal Canadiens also retired his jersey number, 4, in his honor.

Cultural Icon: Beyond his playing career, Béliveau became a beloved figure in Quebec and a symbol of cultural pride, transcending the sport of hockey to become a cultural icon.

These achievements, both in terms of individual accolades and team success, highlight Jean Béliveau's extraordinary impact on the game of hockey and his enduring legacy as one of its greatest ambassadors.

"Respect the game, respect the people that came before you, and you'll get the respect back from the people that come after you."

6

SIDNEY CROSBY

"It doesn't matter what you face; it matters how you face it."

In the little hamlet of Cole Harbour, Nova Scotia, a young kid laced on his skates and skated onto the ice, unsuspecting that he was about to start on a journey that would take him to the peak of the hockey world. Sidney Crosby was that youngster, and his tale is one of unyielding tenacity, amazing skill, and a dedication to perfection that has inspired other young athletes across the world.

The Childhood Years and the Ice-Covered Dream

Sidney Patrick Crosby was born on August 7, 1987, in Cole Harbour, Nova Scotia, a suburb of Halifax. It was evident from the minute he first grabbed a hockey stick that he exhibited a natural knack for the sport. But it wasn't simply his talent that distinguished him; it was his voracious desire to be the best.

Crosby spent numerous hours as a boy on the backyard rink that his father, Troy, painstakingly maintained. The foundations of grandeur were laid on that area of ice. His fantasies of becoming an NHL great were fueled by the harsh cold and the feel of the puck on his stick. His drive was unshakable, and he worked tirelessly toward his objective.

A Hockey Star

Crosby's skill was not overlooked for long. He was already playing in the Quebec Major Junior Hockey League (QMJHL) with the Rimouski Océanic at the age of 16. He scored 135 goals in his second season with the Océanic, exhibiting a level of domination rarely seen in junior hockey.

His phenomenal performance in the QMJHL prepared the path for his NHL debut, but the pressure and expectations were enormous. Many people expected Crosby to be the savior of a faltering NHL team.

Era of the Pittsburgh Penguins

The Pittsburgh Penguins picked Sidney Crosby first overall in the 2005 NHL Entry Draft. It was a historic moment, and the hopes and ambitions of a franchise lay completely on his shoulders.

Crosby did not let us down. He lived up to the huge anticipation in his rookie season, earning the Calder Memorial Trophy as the NHL's Rookie of the Year. In his first season, he scored 102 points, a promising omen of things to come.

But Crosby's path to stardom was not without bumps. Injuries, including a severe concussion, threatened to wreck his career. He overcame each setback, however, with the same dedication that had pushed him from his first days on the rink.

Excellence and Leadership

Sidney Crosby was appointed captain of the Pittsburgh Penguins in 2007, at the age of 19, becoming the NHL's youngest team captain. His leadership on and off the ice was outstanding, and he led his club to many Stanley Cup victories.

Crosby's rigorous work ethic demonstrated his dedication to perfection. He practiced and honed his talents for many hours. His attention to game minutiae, from face-offs to defensive play, distinguishes him as one of the NHL's most complete players.

The Ultimate Goal

One of Crosby's most memorable moments occurred at the 2010 Winter Olympics in Vancouver. Crosby scored the game-winning goal in overtime in the gold medal game against the United States, sealing Canada's Olympic gold medal. It was a moment of national pride, and Crosby's performance on the biggest platform in world hockey cemented his legacy.

Remarkable Comeback

Crosby's trip was not without its challenges. He had a concussion in 2011 that kept him out of the game for an extended amount of time. Many others worried if he would ever be able to play at his old level again. But he beat the odds once more. His remarkable return was a monument to his tenacity and determination to let hardship define his career.

Philanthropy and Community

Sidney Crosby has had a huge influence on the community away from the rink. He's been involved in a number of humanitarian endeavors, including the Sidney Crosby Foundation, which helps youngsters. His donations to the Ronald McDonald House and other charities have won him supporters not just for his talent but also for his character.

Sidney Crosby's path from a little hamlet in Nova Scotia to the pinnacle of the NHL is one that anybody aspiring to greatness can relate to. His commitment, leadership, and capacity to overcome hardship demonstrate the strength of the human spirit. Crosby's impact is more than his great numbers; it is the encouragement he offers to young sportsmen and civilians all across the world. He is a great sports icon, and his tale will be told.ntinue to inspire generations to come.

What did we learn from him?

We may learn from Sidney Crosby that unwavering commitment and persistence are essential factors for success. His unrelenting dedication, even in the face of hardship, proves that losses may be used to propel one to greater heights. Crosby's commitment to continuous improvement reminds us that excellence is the result of consistent work and refining. As the Pittsburgh Penguins' youthful captain, he displays leadership and responsibility, motivating those around him. In the 2010 Olympics, his "Golden Goal" symbolized the strength of representing one's country with pride and sportsmanship. His participation in philanthropy also emphasizes the significance of giving back to the community and leveraging one's success to help others. Overall, Sidney Crosby's tale is a lasting source of inspiration for striving individuals, highlighting that we can achieve extraordinary heights with hard effort, persistence, and a commitment to greatness.

Achievements:

Two-Time Stanley Cup Champion: Crosby led the Pittsburgh Penguins to Stanley Cup victories in 2009 and 2016, cementing his legacy as a franchise player.

Multiple MVP Awards: He has been awarded the Hart Memorial Trophy (NHL's Most Valuable Player) multiple times in his career, underlining his significance in the league.

Art Ross Trophy: Crosby has claimed the Art Ross Trophy as the NHL's leading point-scorer on multiple occasions, showcasing his scoring prowess.

Three-Time Ted Lindsay Award Winner: This award, voted on by the NHL Players' Association, recognizes the most outstanding player in the NHL. Crosby has been honored with this accolade multiple times.

Two-Time Olympic Gold Medalist: Crosby played a pivotal role in securing gold medals for Team Canada in the 2010 and 2014 Winter Olympics.

World Junior Championship Gold: As a young player, he captained Team Canada to a gold medal at the 2005 World Junior Ice Hockey Championships.

Youngest NHL Captain: Crosby became the youngest captain in NHL history when he was named captain of the Pittsburgh Penguins in 2007.

All-Star and All-NHL Team Selections: He has been named to the NHL All-Star Game multiple times and has consistently been selected for the NHL First All-Star Team.

Milestone Achievements: Crosby has reached significant career milestones, including his 1,000th career point in the NHL.

Community and Leadership: Beyond the ice, he is recognized for his philanthropic efforts and his role as a leader on and off the ice.

These accomplishments underscore Sidney Crosby's remarkable career and his indelible mark on the world of hockey. His list of achievements is not only a testament to his exceptional skill but also a reflection of his leadership, determination, and enduring impact on the sport.

"You don't have to be the biggest or the strongest to be successful; you just have to be the most committed."

7

DOMINIK HASEK

"The pursuit of excellence requires relentless dedication, unwavering focus, and the willingness to go beyond what is comfortable or expected."

L egends in ice hockey are created by a unique mix of ability, tenacity, and an unbreakable spirit. Dominik Hasek, a Czech goalie famed for his unconventional and acrobatic technique, engraved his name in the sport's annals by redefining the standards of greatness between the goalposts. Hasek's path from modest beginnings to international renown exemplifies the strength of endurance and determination, demonstrating the heights that may be attained when one refuses to be bound by constraints.

Hasek's enthusiasm for ice hockey began at a young age, when he was born on January 29, 1965, in Pardubice, Czechoslovakia. Hasek's dedication shone clearly despite financial limits and inadequate resources. He started his professional career with the Pardubice Eagles in the Czechoslovak Extraliga. Hasek's exceptional reflexes and unrivaled focus rapidly drew the attention of scouts, resulting in his international debut.

However, the road to prosperity was not without its difficulties. Hasek had multiple setbacks, including injuries and questions about his unconventional playing style. His unconventional approaches were criticized by some as unexpected and unsustainable. However, it was Hasek's unusual ways that became the hallmark of his unprecedented excellence. Rather of complying to expectations, Hasek channeled his unusual qualities, developing them into a lethal weapon that puzzled opponents and gained victories.

Hasek made his long-awaited National Hockey League (NHL) debut with the Chicago Blackhawks in 1990. Despite initial difficulties adjusting to the NHL's rigorous pace, Hasek refused to give up. His persistent dedication to progress led to a move to the Buffalo Sabres, where he truly made his impact. Hasek's acrobatic saves and seemingly impossible stops were legendary in Buffalo, giving him the nickname "The Dominator." His unrivaled work ethic and resilience on and off the ice inspired a generation of ambitious goaltenders, transcending the confines of his sport.

Hasek's defining moment came in the 1998 Nagano Winter Olympics, when he backstopped the Czech Republic to a historic gold medal, demonstrating a masterclass in goaltender prowess that captivated the world's attention. His performance in the gold medal game against Russia, particularly his incredible saves in the shootout, cemented his position as one of the best goaltenders of all time. Hasek's victory in Nagano represented not just a personal success, but also a triumph for the human spirit's tenacity.

His outstanding career concluded in two consecutive Stanley Cup championships with the Detroit Red Wings in 2002 and 2008, where his seasoned leadership and unrivaled talent were instrumental in the team's success. Even in the twilight of his career, Hasek's constant pursuit of excellence served as a beacon of hope for sportsmen throughout the world, underlining that age should never be a barrier to brilliance.

Hasek's humanitarian efforts and dedication to youth development projects in the Czech Republic demonstrated his desire to give back to his community outside of the rink. His construction of hockey schools and camps gave prospective players the resources and guidance they needed to achieve their own aspirations, building a legacy that lasted well beyond his playing career.

Dominik Hasek's imprint on the world of hockey is still felt today. His path from a little hamlet in Czechoslovakia to the summit of world sports shows that excellence has no bounds. Hasek's narrative epitomizes tenacity, determination, and unrelenting pursuit of one's passion. It is a monument to the strength of perseverance and the notion that the impossible can be accomplished with effort and steadfast commitment.

What did we learn from him?

Dominik Hasek's life tells us that genuine success is built via embracing our unique skills and unwavering perseverance, rather than conforming to traditional conventions. Despite initial misgivings and difficulties, Hasek's unconventional playing style proved to be his most valuable asset, establishing the standards of greatness in ice hockey. Even in the face of hardship, his constant dedication to development emphasizes the significance of resilience and tenacity. Hasek's legacy stresses that success is decided not just by conforming to expectations, but also by embracing one's uniqueness and directing it into a force that transcends constraints. He is a source of inspiration, proving that remarkable things can be accomplished with unflinching determination and the willingness to resist traditions.

Achievements:

Two consecutive Hart Memorial Trophies: In 1997 and 1998, Hasek became the first goaltender in history to win the Hart Memorial Trophy, awarded to the NHL's most valuable player.

Six Vezina Trophies: Awarded to the league's best goaltender, Hasek received the Vezina Trophy six times, in 1994, 1995, 1997, 1998, 1999, and 2001, solidifying his status as one of the greatest goaltenders in NHL history.

Olympic Gold Medal: Hasek led the Czech Republic to a historic gold medal at the 1998 Nagano Winter

Olympics, delivering a stunning performance that showcased his exceptional skills and resilience.

Two Stanley Cup Championships: Hasek played an instrumental role in leading the Detroit Red Wings to two Stanley Cup victories, in 2002 and 2008, adding to his legacy as one of the most accomplished goaltenders in the history of the sport.

Induction into the Hockey Hall of Fame: In 2014, Hasek was honored with induction into the Hockey Hall of Fame, solidifying his place among the all-time greats in the world of ice hockey.

These achievements, among others, have cemented Dominik Hasek's legacy as one of the most dominant and influential goaltenders in the history of the sport.

"Success comes from embracing your unique strengths and using them to your advantage, not from conforming to expectations."

8

WAYNE GRETZKY

"You miss 100% of the shots you don't take."

T his iconic quote underscores the importance of seizing opportunities and taking risks in life.

Wayne Gretzky is the personification of brilliance in the world of professional hockey. Gretzky, widely recognized as the greatest hockey player of all time, rose from a backyard rink in Brantford, Ontario, to the peak of the NHL, and his story is nothing short of amazing. His narrative is one of skill, devotion, and the quest of perfection, and it has inspired generations of athletes and fans across the world.

Early Years: Born to Play Hockey

Wayne Douglas Gretzky was born on January 26, 1961, in Brantford, Ontario, Canada. He had a natural knack for hockey from a young age. His father, Walter Gretzky, created a rink in the family's backyard, which became the cradle of Wayne's amazing abilities. Wayne spent numerous hours as a kid developing his stickhandling, shooting, and skating skills on the homemade rink. His father's unfailing support and encouragement nurtured a love for the game that would define his life.

Shattering Records: The Prodigy on Ice

Gretzky's quest to stardom began when he joined the Sault Ste. Marie Greyhounds of the Ontario Hockey League (OHL) at the age of 16. In his debut season, he shattered the record books by scoring an incredible 182 points, a stunning feat for a youngster. His playmaking abilities, vision, and hockey IQ were unrivaled, giving him the moniker "The Great One."

Gretzky continued to break records after joining the Edmonton Oilers in 1979. In his debut season, he scored 51 goals and 137 points, winning him the Hart Memorial Trophy as the league's Most Valuable Player. His points per game average established a new standard that would be unequaled for decades.

Leadership and Championship Success

Gretzky's leadership abilities were on display when he was appointed captain of the Edmonton Oilers in 1983. His ability to motivate and raise his teammates was as impressive as his scoring ability. The Oilers were a dominant force in the NHL during his tenure.

Gretzky led the Oilers to their first Stanley Cup triumph in 1984, bringing the franchise's championship drought to an end. The team's success continued, as they went on to win four more Stanley Cups in the next six seasons. Gretzky's leadership and unwavering pursuit of perfection set the tone for the whole organization.

The Trade Heard Around the World

The hockey world was astonished in 1988 when Wayne Gretzky was traded to the Los Angeles Kings. The "Trade" remains one of the most momentous occurrences in NHL history. Gretzky's influence on hockey stretched well beyond the rink, and his transfer to a non-traditional hockey market in Southern California opened the sport to new audiences.

Gretzky continued to thrive in Los Angeles, hitting milestones that cemented his standing as the NHL's all-time top scorer. He broke Gordie Howe's career point record, leaving an enduring imprint on the game.

The New York Rangers' Return to Glory

Gretzky's career came full circle in 1996, when he joined the New York Rangers. During his three seasons with the Rangers, he once again shown his lasting skill and leadership, finally securing his final trip in the Stanley Cup Finals.

Beyond the Ice: Impact and Inspiration

Wayne Gretzky's effect on hockey goes well beyond his numbers. His devotion, sportsmanship, and passion for the game have left an unforgettable impression on the sport. His accomplishments and awards, which include four Stanley Cups and nine Hart Trophies, place him in a class by themselves. However, it is his temperament, humility, and passion for the game that make him a great role model and inspiration to innumerable young players.

Leadership and Insight: As a captain, Gretzky exemplified what it takes to lead with elegance, humility, and commitment.

What did we learn from him?

Wayne Gretzky's life story is inspirational. His unwavering pursuit of greatness inspires us to strive for constant development. His humble and unselfish leadership teaches us that genuine greatness is found in boosting others. Gretzky's influence goes beyond statistics, emphasizing the value of character and sportsmanship. His relocation to the Los Angeles Kings broadens our views, demonstrating how common interests may unite people from different cultures. His unwavering humility motivates us to think that true greatness is manifested not just in talent but also in how we treat people and deal with achievement. Gretzky's path is a source of inspiration for everybody.

Achievements:

All-Time Leading Scorer: Gretzky holds the record for the most career points in NHL history, with an astounding 2,857 points.

Hart Trophies: He won the Hart Memorial Trophy (NHL's Most Valuable Player) an incredible nine times, showcasing his impact on the league.

Stanley Cup Championships: Gretzky led the Edmonton Oilers to four Stanley Cup championships during the 1980s, establishing the team as a dynasty.

Assists Record: He holds the record for the most career assists in NHL history, with 1,963.

Scoring Titles: Gretzky claimed the Art Ross Trophy as the league's leading point-scorer on ten occasions.

Lester B. Pearson/Ted Lindsay Award: He was named the NHL's outstanding player as voted by his fellow players on five occasions.

Lady Byng Trophies: Gretzky's sportsmanship on the ice earned him the Lady Byng Trophy on five occasions.

Record-Setting Season: In the 1985-1986 season, he set single-season records for goals (92) and points (215).

Achievements Beyond Numbers: Gretzky's impact extended far beyond statistics, as he changed the way the game was played and introduced new strategies and tactics.

Legacy: His lasting legacy is his influence on the sport and his ability to inspire generations of hockey players and fans.

Wayne Gretzky's achievements not only define his incredible career but also serve as a benchmark of excellence in the world of professional sports.

"You have to believe in yourself when no one else does. That makes you a winner right there."

9

PETER FORSBER

"Play every game like it's your last, and you'll leave a legacy worth remembering."

The narrative of Peter Forsberg's rise to hockey stardom is one of unflinching dedication, incredible skill, and everlasting commitment. This Swedish hockey icon, noted for his superb two-way play and fierce leadership, is more than simply a great athlete; he is an inspiration. His journey to NHL greatness was anything but average, with trials that challenged his toughness and integrity. Forsberg's life exemplifies what can be accomplished with passion, determination, and an unbreakable spirit.

The Beginnings of the Hockey Dream

Peter Forsberg was born in Örnsköldsvik, Sweden, on July 20, 1973. His father, Kent Forsberg, was a former Swedish national team player, thus his early exposure to hockey was unsurprising. The game captivated little Peter, and the rink became his second home. His father's advice and the family's constant support were important in developing his skill.

Forsberg left his birthplace at the age of 16 to chase his passion, joining the Modo Hockey team in Sweden's premier league, the Elitserien. His remarkable performances with Modo drew the attention of scouts from all across the world.

The Colorado Avalanche's NHL Debut

The Philadelphia Flyers selected Peter Forsberg with the sixth overall choice in the NHL Entry Draft in 1991. His NHL career, however, began in earnest when he was moved to the Quebec Nordiques, who would eventually become the Colorado Avalanche. With Forsberg's arrival in Colorado, an era of domination began.

His early NHL years were nothing short of remarkable. Forsberg's ability, grit, and determination made him an immediate sensation. He helped lead the Avalanche to their first Stanley Cup in 1995-1996, receiving the Conn Smythe Trophy as the playoffs' most valuable player.

Triumphs and setbacks: The Injury-Racked Road

While Forsberg's abilities were evident, his path was far from easy. Injuries to his feet and ankles, in particular, began to plague him. Despite undergoing major operations, his unrelenting commitment saw him return to the rink each time, impressing spectators with his tenacity.

His return to the Stanley Cup Finals in 2001 was maybe one of his most memorable experiences. Forsberg made a stunning return in the finals after missing much of the regular season and playoffs due to injuries. His presence and leadership were vital in the Avalanche winning their second Stanley Cup. This extraordinary display of willpower demonstrated Forsberg's capacity to overcome hardship.

Legacy of an Avalanche Icon in Colorado

Forsberg's tenure with the Colorado Avalanche was distinguished by his continuous excellence. His extraordinary skill set, which combined playmaking ability with physical presence, won him admirers and teammates alike. He was known as "Foppa" and was regarded as one of the franchise's all-time greats.

Forsberg's influence went beyond the rink as one of the team's leaders. His work ethic, humility, and sportsmanship serve as role models for younger athletes. In the late 1990s and early 2000s, he was a driving influence behind the Avalanche's success.

Gold Medals and National Pride: International Glory

Forsberg's influence extended beyond the NHL. He was a vital component for the Swedish national team on the international level. His efforts in the Winter Olympics and World Championships earned him gold medals at the Lillehammer Winter Olympics in 1994 and the Turin Olympics in 2006.

His enthusiasm for supporting his country shone through in every step he took on the world stage. He became a national icon and an inspiration to young Swedish hockey players.

Retirement and Swan Song

Forsberg's playing career came to a halt as injuries continued to haunt him. He briefly returned to the Colorado Avalanche and the Nashville Predators, but it was evident that his body could no longer endure the demands of professional hockey. He announced his retirement from the NHL in 2011.

What did we learn from him?

The life and work of Peter Forsberg provide tremendous insights and inspiration. His ability to overcome crippling injuries shows us the value of perseverance in the face of adversity. His tenacity to rise each time he fell is a monument to the unchanging strength of the human spirit. Forsberg proved, both on and off the ice, that genuine leadership is defined by actions, not just words. His humility, work ethic, and devotion serve as a model for his colleagues and aspiring sportsmen. His desire to represent Sweden at the world level emphasizes the dignity and pride that comes from representing one's country. His commitment to his national team exemplifies the ideals of devotion and patriotism.

Despite his extraordinary talent and success, Forsberg remained modest and sportsmanlike, acting as a shining example of how a professional athlete should behave oneself. His unwavering love for the game and devotion to constant growth highlight the value of dedication and hard effort in reaching excellence. Forsberg's enduring effect on the Colorado Avalanche, as well as the passion with which fans and the franchise remember him, demonstrate the immense impact a single man can have on a club and a city. His amazing path exemplifies resilience, leadership, national pride, humility, enthusiasm, and devotion.

Achievements:

Two-time Stanley Cup Champion: Forsberg played an integral role in the Colorado Avalanche's Stanley Cup victories in 1996 and 2001.

Calder Memorial Trophy: He was named the NHL's Rookie of the Year in 1995, showcasing his immediate impact on the league.

Art Ross Trophy: Forsberg won the NHL scoring title during the 2002-2003 season, underscoring his offensive prowess.

Hart Memorial Trophy: He received the league's Most Valuable Player award for the 2002-2003 season.

Two Olympic Gold Medals: Forsberg was a key contributor to Sweden's gold medal victories at the 1994 Lillehammer Olympics and the 2006 Turin Olympics.

World Championships: He helped Sweden secure multiple gold medals in the IIHF World Championships.

IIHF Triple Gold Club: Forsberg is part of this exclusive group of players who have won an Olympic gold medal, a World Championship, and a Stanley Cup.

All-Star Selections: He was a frequent NHL All-Star, showcasing his consistent excellence.

Swedish Hockey Hall of Fame: Forsberg was inducted into the Swedish Hockey Hall of Fame in recognition of his contributions to the sport.

Legacy: His lasting legacy is as one of the most beloved and revered players in the history of the Colorado Avalanche and in the hearts of hockey fans around the world.

"Leadership isn't about being the loudest voice in the room; it's about being the one who leads by example."

10

ALEXANDER OVECHKIN

"Set your goals high, work hard, and never stop believing in yourself. That's the recipe for greatness."

Alexander Ovechkin, also known as "Ovi" and "The Great 8," is more than a hockey player. He is an icon, a source of inspiration, and one of the best goal scorers in National Hockey League (NHL) history. His path from a little child in Moscow, Russia, to becoming a hockey icon is one of passion, tenacity, and the pursuit of a goal that crosses borders and languages.

Childhood and Family History

Ovechkin was born in Moscow, Russia, on September 17, 1985. His family has a strong connection to the sport of hockey. Tatyana Ovechkina, his mother, is a two-time Olympic gold winner in basketball, and his father, Mikhail Ovechkin, is a professional soccer player. With such a sporty lineage, it seemed natural for young Alexander to pursue an athletic career.

Hockey quickly captivated his heart. His older brother Sergei gave him his first hockey stick when he was two years old. This little act sparked a passion that would shape the rest of his life.

Russia's Hockey Factory

Hockey is more than a sport in Russia; it's a way of life. Young boys and girls lace up their skates and head out onto the ice, hoping to become the next major hockey star. Ovechkin was no different. He belonged to an age that revered Russian greats like Pavel Bure and Igor Larionov, and he aspired to be like them.

Ovechkin spent his early years developing his abilities in the Russian youth divisions. He was a member of Dynamo Moscow, one of Russia's most illustrious clubs. His talent became more obvious as he developed. He distinguished out for his amazing shooting, quickness, and almost limitless energy.

Making a Name for Oneself in the NHL Draft

The young Russian prodigy's name was on everyone's lips when the NHL held its annual draft in 2004. The Washington Capitals had the first overall pick, and Ovechkin was regarded the top prospect. The stakes were extremely high, but Ovechkin was ready to take on the world.

His travel from Russia to America was a watershed point in his life. It wasn't simply a cross-country move; it was a leap of faith into the unknown. The language, culture, and playing style were all distinct. But Ovechkin was unfazed. He was on a quest to show himself on hockey's grandest stage.

A Freshman Sensation

Ovechkin's first NHL season was nothing short of spectacular. He finished the season with 52 goals and

54 assists, winning him the Calder Memorial Trophy as the league's best rookie. His playing technique was sensational. He was noted for his lightning-fast speed, bone-crushing body checks, and a blast that ripped through goaltenders' gloves. In Washington, he instantly became a fan favorite.

Personal and Professional Difficulties

Despite his early success, Ovechkin had personal difficulties. Sergei, his younger brother, died suddenly at the age of 24. Ovechkin was devastated by his brother's death and dedicated his career to his memory. This personal sorrow only increased his ambition to achieve in hockey.

Ovechkin was a force to be reckoned with on the ice, but the Capitals failed to make long postseason runs. Year after year, they were disappointed, and Ovechkin was frequently chastised for his team's failure to win the Stanley Cup. The weight of expectations and the voices of naysayers only fueled his determination.

Leading the Capitals to Victory

Ovechkin's leadership abilities were evident, and he was elected Capitals captain in 2010. He welcomed the challenge with the same zeal he shown on the rink. His leadership inspired the club, and the Capitals won their first Stanley Cup in 2018. The moment Ovechkin lifted the Cup was emotional and memorable. He had silenced his detractors. fulfilled his lifelong dream.

What did we learn from him?

His relentless devotion to hockey tells us that dedication and love for our endeavors are essential for reaching excellence. Ovechkin's bravery in the face of personal sorrow displays the ability to overcome life's most difficult challenges.

His willingness to embrace change and adapt to new difficulties exemplifies the benefits of moving outside of our comfort zones. On the ice, Ovechkin's transformational leadership emphasizes the importance of cooperation and encouraging others to strive toward common goals.

His reluctance to give up in the face of adversity serves as a poignant reminder of the benefits of perseverance. Achieving lifelong aspirations, like he did with the Stanley Cup, emphasizes the significance of identifying and pursuing our most treasured objectives.

Ovechkin's ability to bring civilizations together via athletics demonstrates the universality of human connection. His record-breaking success proves that constant hard effort can lead to spectacular results.

Achievements:

Multiple Rocket Richard Trophies: Ovechkin has won the Maurice "Rocket" Richard Trophy as the NHL's top goal-scorer multiple times, showcasing his unparalleled scoring ability.

Three Hart Memorial Trophies: His three MVP awards underscore his significant impact on the league and his team.

Art Ross Trophy: Winning the NHL scoring title emphasizes his all-around offensive capabilities.

Stanley Cup Champion: Leading the Washington Capitals to their first Stanley Cup championship in 2018 was a career-defining moment.

All-Star Appearances: Ovechkin has been selected to numerous NHL All-Star Games, highlighting his consistent excellence.

Over 700 Career Goals: His goal-scoring prowess places him among the greatest in the history of the sport.

Multiple 50-Goal Seasons: Achieving 50 goals or more in a single season multiple times is a remarkable feat.

Franchise Icon: Ovechkin's legacy in Washington goes beyond statistics; he is an icon in the franchise's history.

Cultural Impact: His ability to bridge the gap between Russian and North American hockey culture is a testament to his influence on the global game.

Ovechkin's achievements are a reflection of his exceptional talent, dedication, and consistency in the sport of hockey. He has left an indelible mark on the NHL and the hearts of hockey fans around the world.

"Passion fuels excellence. Love what you do, and you'll do it with heart."

11

CONNOR MCDAVID

"Perseverance is the key to achieving your goals; it's about staying focused on your path, even when the journey gets tough."

F ew names in professional ice hockey elicit as much respect and affection as Connor McDavid. McDavid, a tremendous talent from an early age, has cemented his position among the sport's all-time greats with his relentless devotion, incredible skill, and genuine passion for the game. His path from a tiny hamlet in Ontario to the worldwide stage of the National Hockey League (NHL) is proof of the power of unyielding dedication and the pursuit of perfection.

McDavid's interest for the sport began when he was a toddler in Richmond Hill, Ontario, Canada, on January 13, 1997. His exceptional aptitude and instinctive grasp of the game set him apart from his contemporaries even at a young age. He led the Erie Otters of the Ontario Hockey League (OHL) as a youngster, where his outstanding speed, vision, and scoring ability garnered him significant acclaim as a once-in-a-generation talent. McDavid's quest to greatness actually began during this period, as he mastered the demands of professional athletics with a maturity and composure that belied his age.

McDavid's entry into the NHL was welcomed with great expectations when the Edmonton Oilers picked him with the first overall choice in the 2015 NHL Entry Draft. Despite the weight of expectation, McDavid remained unwavering, approaching each game with unwavering intensity and an insatiable desire for victory. His remarkable speed, unrivaled playmaking skills, and unwavering desire rapidly established him as a league force to be reckoned with.

His ascension, however, was not without difficulties. During his debut season, a serious injury threatened to derail his momentum, casting doubt on his ability to return to peak form. Despite this, McDavid's tenacity shined through as he went through rigorous recovery and training, emerging stronger and more resilient than ever. His incredible return demonstrated not just his athletic brilliance, but also his unshakeable mental toughness and tenacity in the face of adversity.

McDavid's effect on the sport grew beyond numbers as his career developed. He became a symbol of hope and inspiration for young athletes all around the world, demonstrating that even the most lofty of aspirations can be accomplished with unflinching devotion and a rigorous work ethic. His dedication to self-improvement, both on and off the ice, established a standard of excellence that encouraged a generation of young hockey players to reach their full potential.

McDavid won the Art Ross Trophy in 2017, after leading the league in points and establishing himself as one of the NHL's top players. Following that, he was chosen captain of the Edmonton Oilers, becoming him the franchise's youngest captain. His leadership on and off the ice, along with his excellent skill set, invigorated the squad and instilled in the organization a revitalized spirit of conviction and desire.

McDavid's attention to community engagement and humanitarian initiatives, in addition to his individual accomplishments, emphasized his determination to having a good effect beyond of the rink. His engagement in many programs aimed at encouraging young sports participation and aiding local communities underscored his confidence in leveraging his position to make significant change and inspire the next generation of athletes.

Connor McDavid's influence is being felt across the hockey world today. His journey from a tiny hamlet in Canada to the pinnacle of worldwide celebrity serves as a poignant reminder that the seemingly impossible can be accomplished with steadfast dedication, uncompromising tenacity, and an unwavering enthusiasm for one's work. McDavid's tale represents the spirit of tenacity, determination, and constant pursuit of perfection, providing as a source of inspiration for sportsmen and dreamers worldwide.

Connor McDavid is a paragon of tenacity in the ever-changing environment of professional sports, taking the sport of ice hockey to new heights and leaving an unforgettable impression on the hearts and minds of fans and aspiring athletes worldwide. His story is a monument to the transformational power of tenacity and the notion that greatness is within grasp with effort and an unflinching commitment to one's purpose.

What did we learn from him?

The path of Connor McDavid teaches us the transformational force of resilience, persistence, and the tireless pursuit of perfection. His ability to overcome failures and injuries demonstrates the value of tenacity in the face of adversity. McDavid's leadership abilities and dedication to team unity highlight the importance of cultivating a healthy team culture. Furthermore, his participation in community service programs emphasizes the importance of leveraging one's position to benefit society. Overall, McDavid's narrative serves as a compelling reminder that even the most lofty of aspirations can be accomplished with unshakable devotion, tenacity, and a passion for one's art.

Achievements:

Art Ross Trophy: McDavid won the Art Ross Trophy in the NHL in the 2016-2017 and 2017-2018 seasons, leading the league in total points during those years.

Hart Memorial Trophy: He was awarded the Hart Memorial Trophy in the 2016-2017 season, recognizing him as the most valuable player in the NHL.

Ted Lindsay Award: McDavid received the Ted Lindsay Award, formerly known as the Lester B. Pearson Award, in the 2016-2017 and 2017-2018 seasons, as the most outstanding player in the NHL as voted by the NHL Players' Association.

NHL All-Star Team Selections: He has been selected to the NHL All-Star Team multiple times during his career, showcasing his consistent performance and skill at the highest level of the sport.

McDavid's achievements have solidified his place as one of the premier players in the NHL, and he continues to be recognized for his exceptional contributions to the sport.

"Success is not just about talent; it's about the relentless dedication to honing your craft and pushing past your limits."

12

AUSTON MATTHEWS

"Work hard, stay positive, and get up early. It's the best part of the day."

Auston Matthews is one of the most well-known names in professional ice hockey. Matthews' road to international success has been marked by an unyielding devotion to greatness, a magnificent display of skill, and an indomitable personality that has grabbed the hearts of fans all around the world. From modest origins to advancement to the ranks of the National Hockey League (NHL), Matthews' tale exemplifies the transformational force of tenacity, determination, and an undying enthusiasm for the game.

Auston Matthews, who was born on September 17, 1997, in San Ramon, California, showed an early interest in the game. Matthews' journey began at the local rinks of Scottsdale, Arizona, where he refined his talents and gained a fundamental grasp of the game, where he was raised in a family that encouraged his passion for hockey. Despite growing up in a non-traditional hockey market, Matthews' talent and devotion came through, laying the groundwork for an extraordinary rise to the summit of professional hockey.

Matthews' path to the NHL was not without difficulties. As a young player in a non-hockey-centric region of Arizona, he experienced doubts about his ability to compete at the highest level. His unwavering commitment and unrivaled work ethic, on the other hand, spurred him ahead, driving him up the levels of junior hockey and cementing his status as a top prospect for the NHL Entry Draft.

Matthews' aspirations came true in 2016 when the Toronto Maple Leafs selected him as the first overall choice in the NHL Entry Draft. His sensational NHL debut season, in which he scored four goals in his first game, marked his entrance on the great stage of professional hockey. Matthews' tremendous scoring ability, paired with his outstanding on-ice vision and playmaking abilities, rapidly established him as a league force to be reckoned with.

Matthews has faced difficulties on several occasions throughout his career. Injuries and disappointments taxed his fortitude, but his ability to overcome these obstacles with unrelenting resolve and an unyielding devotion to his trade cemented his image as a real contender. His fortitude in the face of adversity serves as a compelling reminder that setbacks are not barriers to progress and self-improvement, but rather chances for growth and self-improvement.

Matthews' influence goes beyond his individual accomplishments on the ice. He has utilized his position as a prominent person in the hockey world to encourage the next generation of players, emphasizing the significance of hard work, perseverance, and a persistent pursuit of one's goals. His engagement in community projects and youth development programs demonstrates his dedication to give back and making a good difference in both the sport and the larger community.

Auston Matthews' legacy continues to excite hockey fans all over the world. His path from the rinks of Arizona to the international limelight shows the transformational power of determination and hard work. Matthews' tale is a light of hope, reminding us that even the most lofty of aspirations can be accomplished with unyielding perseverance, a rigorous work ethic, and an enduring enthusiasm for one's trade.

Auston Matthews stands as a tribute to the resiliency of the human spirit in an ever-changing context of professional athletics, exhibiting the essence of persistence and the relentless pursuit of perfection. His journey serves as a compelling reminder that the impossible can be accomplished with perseverance, devotion, and a passion for one's trade.

What did we learn from him?

We discover the transformational force of tenacity, determination, and the dogged pursuit of perfection from Auston Matthews. His story reminds us that success is defined not by circumstances, but by an individual's everlasting dedication to their art. Matthews' tenacity in the face of doubt and disappointments illustrates the value of perseverance in accomplishing one's goals. His model of leadership emphasizes the need of motivating others through hard work and perseverance. Furthermore, his participation in community efforts emphasizes the need of giving back and using one's position to effect positive change. Overall, Matthews' tale serves as a compelling reminder that even the most difficult difficulties can be overcome with determination, persistence, and a passion for one's work.

Achievement:

Calder Memorial Trophy: Matthews received the Calder Memorial Trophy in 2017, recognizing him as the NHL's rookie of the year.

Maurice "Rocket" Richard Trophy: He won the Maurice "Rocket" Richard Trophy in the 2019-2020 NHL season, awarded to the league's top goal-scorer.

NHL All-Star Team Selections: Matthews has been selected to the NHL All-Star Team multiple times, showcasing his consistent performance and impact in the league.

Selection as the first overall pick in the NHL Entry Draft: His selection as the first overall pick in the 2016 NHL Entry Draft by the Toronto Maple Leafs highlighted his status as a highly regarded and talented prospect.

2022 All Star selection
2022 Hart Memorial trophy Winner
2022 Ted Lindsey Award Winner

"You have to have that drive and that determination to want to be better every day and want to improve."

CONCLUSION

And so, we reach the end of our incredible journey, filled with the inspiring tales of our hockey heroes. Their stories have taught us that with passion, perseverance, and teamwork, we can conquer any challenge that comes our way. Just like our favorite players on the ice, we too can score our own goals and achieve our dreams, no matter how big they may seem.

When things seem tough, and it feels like giving up is the only option, let's remember the courage and determination of these amazing athletes. They showed us that with hard work and a positive attitude, we can overcome any obstacle that stands in our way. They remind us that it's okay to make mistakes, as long as we learn from them and keep moving forward.

As we bid farewell to these captivating stories, let's hold on to the lessons they taught us. Let's never forget the importance of believing in ourselves, supporting our friends, and being part of a team. Let's always remember that even when the going gets tough, we have what it takes to rise to the challenge and emerge victorious.

So, let's lace up our imaginary skates, take to the ice of life, and show the world what we're made of! With a little determination, a dash of teamwork, and a whole lot of heart, we can glide through life's ups and downs and score our own winning goals, just like our hockey heroes. The final buzzer may have sounded, but our own adventures are just beginning!

Made in the USA
Middletown, DE
02 June 2024

55158780R00060